The Missing Charango

Ann Weil

Illustrated by Brooke Scudder

Rigby®

For the past two weeks during music class, Oscar and his classmates had been studying instruments from around the world.

"That was an example of African drumming," said their music teacher, turning off the CD player. "Next time we'll listen to folk music from South America."

instruments from around the world

"My dad's from South America, and he plays folk music on an instrument called a charango," Oscar said when Ms. Hamilton called on him. "I could bring it in on Wednesday."

"What's a charango?" asked Oscar's friend Louis.

"It's an instrument with strings that looks like a tiny guitar," Oscar replied.

"That would be great!" Ms. Hamilton exclaimed.

Oscar was about to leave his house on Wednesday morning when he remembered the charango.

"Dad, is it OK if I take your charango to school?" Oscar yelled, but there was no answer.

"He must have gone to work already. Mom is in the shower, and Grandma and Grandpa went to the market, so I can't ask them," Oscar thought as he lifted the charango case off the shelf.

SCHOOL BUS

Oscar knew that the charango was special because it had been a gift from his father's best friend Miguel. For a moment, Oscar considered whether Dad would want him to take it to school.

Glancing out the window, Oscar saw that the school bus was coming, so he had to decide immediately. The bus would drop him off at 4:00 that afternoon, and his father didn't get home from work until 5:30. Oscar thought that he could take the charango and return it before his father even knew that it was gone.

When Oscar tried to put the charango into his overstuffed backpack, he realized that it wouldn't fit. He decided to just carry the charango in the case. That way it wouldn't get broken. Then he rushed outside to catch the bus.

That afternoon during music class, Oscar showed everyone the charango. "People used to make these instruments out of armadillo shells," he said.

"That's amazing!" exclaimed Louis.

After everyone had a chance to look at the charango and hear how it sounded, Oscar placed it on the table next to the CD player.

music from
South America

"Thank you, Oscar," said Ms. Hamilton. "Now class, let's listen for the sound of the charango in this folk music played by people who live in South America."

When music class was over, Oscar grabbed the charango case and rushed to be first in line, completely forgetting about the charango.

After school, Oscar's backpack was really heavy, so he asked Louis if he would carry the charango case. When Louis picked it up he said, "This charango case is as light as a feather."

"Oh no!" said Oscar taking the case from Louis and opening it. "The charango case is empty! I have to find the charango!"

"The bus is about to leave," Louis said.

Oscar realized that he couldn't look for the charango or he'd miss the bus. Then he'd have to explain the missing charango to his parents.

Worried, Oscar followed Louis onto the bus.

Oscar could hardly eat his dinner that night because he was so worried about the missing instrument.

"Miguel called earlier to tell us that he'll be here by 5:00 tomorrow evening," said Grandma with a smile on her face.

Suddenly Oscar sat up straight and listened. Whenever Miguel came to visit, Dad took out his charango, and the two men played folk music together.

"Aren't you hungry?" Grandma asked Oscar.

He shook his head. It made Oscar feel sick just thinking about the look on Dad's face when he found out that the charango was missing.

Oscar went to bed right after dinner but didn't fall asleep because he was thinking about the charango. He knew that his father would be very angry with him for taking the instrument without permission and even more upset that Oscar had lost it.

Mom came into his room the next morning, already dressed for work. "You don't look well," she said to Oscar. "I think that you should stay home with Grandma today."

Oscar, worried about finding the charango before Miguel arrived, said that he was fine.

"You should stay in bed today and rest," Mom said firmly.

That evening when Miguel arrived, Oscar answered the door.

"Hello," Miguel said to Oscar.

When they sat down to eat dinner, Miguel described a new film that he had read about in the newspaper.

"It would be fun to see a movie tonight," said Mom.

"Grandpa and I can stay here with Oscar," suggested Grandma.

Oscar was relieved. If Dad and Miguel went to the movies, they wouldn't play folk music that night, and no one would notice that the charango was missing. Smiling for the first time that day, Oscar ate his dinner and even asked for more!

When Oscar arrived at school on Friday, he hurried into his classroom and greeted his teacher.

"Good morning, Oscar," said Mr. Phillips. "We all missed you yesterday."

"Have you seen my charango?" Oscar asked hopefully.

"Didn't you take it to music class on Wednesday?"

"Oh, now I remember. May I please
go to the music room to look for it?"
Oscar asked.

Mr. Phillips nodded, and Oscar raced
down the hall to the music room. The
classroom was empty, and Oscar quickly ran
over to the table where he remembered
putting the charango. It wasn't there!

Oscar didn't notice Ms. Hamilton until she was standing right next to him. "Is this what you're looking for?" she asked with a big smile, holding out the charango.

"Thank you so much!" Oscar exclaimed, giving his music teacher a big smile.

"Your charango was left on the table after Wednesday's class, and I kept it locked inside my office," she explained as Oscar took the instrument. "I looked for you yesterday to return it, but your teacher said that you were sick at home. Are you feeling better today?"

Oscar nodded and smiled again. No one had ever felt as happy as he!

Since Oscar had left the case at home, he carefully wrapped his sweatshirt around the charango and placed it in his empty school bag. Then he put the bag on a shelf in his locker where it would be safe until it was time to go home.

As Oscar hopped off the bus that afternoon, he noticed that his father's car was already in the driveway. Oscar ran into the house, but he was too late. He saw Miguel holding his instrument, and Dad was reaching for the charango case.

"No, Dad, it's not in there!"

"Where is my charango?" Dad asked as he opened the empty case.

Oscar took the charango out of his bag and handed it to his father. Then Oscar told him the whole story. "I'll never take anything without asking again," he promised.

"Thank you for telling the truth," Dad said. "Now let's play some music!"